God, Where Is My Husband? 10 Things To Know While You Wait

God, Where Is My Husband?
10 Things To Know While You Wait

Kacie Starr Long

Dedication

First and foremost I dedicate this book to my Lord and Savior Jesus Christ, who breathed His mighty wind through me and allowed me to write this book. I thank the Lord for every test, trial, and now the victory to help encourage other Christian women, so they too can know that God is faithful.

I want to thank my lovely mother, Jill Triplett, for her support, love and prayers. As a teenager, I watched her get up early to pray for her family. I am the woman in Christ due to her prayers.

To my wonderful, God-sent and fearing husband who was brought to me after applying the wisdom and revelation given to me by God during my singleness...Min. Alfred T. Long, Sr., I LOVE YOU! Thank you for encouraging me to birth this book, especially during the times I was ready to give up. You were worth the wait!

I finally want to acknowledge every prophetic voice that spoke this book into existence. I encountered so many prophetic men and women who spoke a "thus saith the Lord" concerning this book and encouraged me throughout my singleness. May you always speak words seasoned with salt and grace.

Contents

Introduction

---❖---

This book has been in the works for a long season, but you know how it can be with an extended project -- you start, get sidetracked by another project stop, and then start once again. I always knew God wanted me to write a book for Christian singles, but it wasn't until my friend, LaTonya, called me up to say that the Lord was displeased with my lack of discipline concerning this book that I finally put my foot to the metal to finish.

Don't get me wrong, it wasn't that I didn't want to write this book for you to enjoy, but "life" just seemed to get in the way. I pray that by reading this book, you come to understand how much purpose and destiny God has inside YOU so you too can be aware of the distractions and temptations presented by "life" and instead will plow forward and complete every assignment God has for you.

I believe everyone has a book inside of him or her, and it's up to you to decide whether or not you will bring it to birth. This book has been written out of direct obedience to our Father God, to tell the world that He *does* hear the prayers of His people and He is constantly at work to answer our prayers and bring them to manifestation. It is my hope that by reading this book, your faith will be increased and produce lasting fruit in your life.

For so many years, I believed earnestly that God would send me my husband. I had no idea who or where he was but, by faith, *I believed God.* I knew that He was making a God-fearing man that was custom made just for me and in His perfect timing, we would meet. It wasn't always easy waiting, but I can look back and see how God was with me every step of the way.

May this book encourage and inspire you to trust and wait on God. And, while you wait, may you become equipped and prepared to be the godly wife God has called you to be. May you always remember.....

The LORD your God is with you, the Mighty Warrior who saves. He will take great delight in you; in his love he will no longer rebuke you, but will rejoice over you with singing." – Zephaniah 3:17

"Come to Me, all who are weary and heavy-laden, and I will give you rest. Take my yoke upon you and learn from Me, for I am gentle and humble in heart, and you will find rest for your soul. For my yoke is easy and my burden is light."
Matthew 11:28-30

CHAPTER 1

Wait Well With Patience

Be patient, then, brothers and sisters, until the Lord's coming. See how the farmer waits for the land to yield its valuable crop, patiently waiting for the autumn and spring rains.

James 5:7

Prophetess Juanita Bynum released a heartfelt song a few years ago entitled, "I Don't Mind Waiting." In the song she beautifully sings unto the Lord stating her willingness to wait on God's perfect timing. She even mentions how much of an honor it is to wait on God. I've always enjoyed Prophetess Bynum's fiery preaching but for a long time I detested her song. That "waiting song" is what I called it.

Honestly, God.... I would think. *Who actually likes to wait for things to happen? They must be out of their mind!* Unlike Prophetess Bynum, many days during my singleness, I *DID* mind waiting. I was tired of waiting on God to send me my husband and I wanted him to appear quickly.

God, what is taking so long? I often wondered.

GOD KNOWS BEST

Perhaps you feel the same way and are often bombarded with feelings of impatience and frustration regarding God's responsiveness to your prayers and desires; however, be encouraged. 2 Peter 3:9 informs us that God is "not slow in keeping his promises as some understand slowness" yet He is patient with us and, allows the time for us to evolve with our circumstances, so we are equipped and prepared to receive what He has for us. After all, there is nothing worse than receiving a blessing for which you are ill equipped and unprepared. In my professional career, I reached great heights very quickly. At one point I served as the youngest politician ever elected in the history of St. Louis, Missouri.

I hosted a local television show, I participated in international delegations to Europe and Asia, oversaw millions of dollars in construction and development in my legislative district, and served as the local spokesperson for Barack Obama's first presidential campaign. God had blessed me with much, all at the tender age of 26, yet I was unequipped emotionally to manage and maintain these blessings. The spirits of pride and arrogance swelled along with the equally duplicitous spirits of lust of power and temptation.

Everything came crashing down several years later when I publicly admitted to stealing money designated for my political campaign and instead used it to fund my personal lifestyle of expensive hair weaves, nails and nice restaurants. God had placed me in a position to speak up for those in need, to create laws of fairness and justice, and to use my influence as a popular politician to help His people, but my immaturity, greed and sin proved that my character was not up for the task. Despite the votes of approval and confidence placed in me by the public, I showed just how much I fell short of the hype, buzz noted in my campaign literature as God exposed my inner character, lack of integrity and spiritual shallowness. As a single woman you may feel like you are ready to get married and in a rush to meet and fall in love with your future husband; however, know that God's timing is impeccable. He knows exactly what you are ready for and when you are ready for it. Learn to wait well on Him with patience.

LEARN HOW TO WAIT WELL

So, how do you wait well with patience? The first thing you do is ask God for patience. Often times God is ready to give us exactly what we need, but we fail to ask Him. "We have not because we ask not." (James 4:3)

One day during my worship time when that "waiting song" began to play, I prayed to God to have the attitude of Juanita Bynum. *"Lord, let me truly not mind waiting on you."* I was tired of being impatient. I was tired of wondering, hoping and assuming that the next guy I came across would be my husband. The thoughts, and anxiety about "is he the one" was wearing me thin. I desired peace and I needed relief from the agony and consternation produced by my impatience. Slowly, but surely He answered them and I was able to confess the scripture found in James 1:4 with sincerity.

But let patience have its perfect work that you may be perfect and complete, lacking nothing.

Despite my patience, I knew as a single that I wanted to be spiritually full and complete; I didn't want to lack in any area of my life, especially concerning the marriage God had for me. I wanted God to use my singleness for His glory and to fully prepare and mold me for all the great things He had in store.

God wants you to get to the place where you will yield your plans, your thoughts, and your dreams to *His* will for your life. If it had been up to me and my plans for life, I would still be a politician, married to a rich attorney and have 2.5 kids with a German shepherd dog in the backyard; however that was not God's plan for my life. We must be willing to submit our plans for God's will and allow Him to direct our course. When we refuse to submit and attempt to take matters in our hands, disaster is always on the horizon.

IMPATIENCE BREEDS DISASTER

Let's look at the story of Sarah and Abraham as an example. God promised Abraham that he would be the father of many nations. Yet, he and Sarah were old and had no children. As time passed they both grew impatient and decided to take matters into their own hands. At the urging of his wife, Abraham slept with his wife's maid, Hagar, and produced a son, named Ishmael.

Sarah and Abraham's impatience and lack of respect for God's timetable and plan resulted in drama, confusion and tension that ultimately caused pain and separation. Abraham was required to send Hagar and Ishmael away forever with the clothes on their backs and just a bit of bread and water to sustain them. When we refuse to wait on God and attempt to work things out through our flesh, because we feel like *now* is the time for something to happen, the results often wind up like Hagar's bread and water– hardly sustaining. Alternatively, when we wait on God, He provides everything we need and we are able to live under His divine covering and protection.

I remember being so excited about this young preacher that had expressed interest in me. He was tall, handsome, articulate and a great writer. I had been single for what felt like forever and had been praying and actively seeking God for a husband, so when the preacher expressed interest in me, I just *knew* that he was the one! My impatience caused me to miss all the warning signs.

For example there was his multiple children out of wedlock, his comments and beliefs about fornication and sexual immorality that didn't line up with scripture, his emotional distance and repeated failed attempts with keeping his promises.

My flesh was fueled by my impatience. I tried to unrealistically fit a square peg into a round hole. I assessed the relationship from all sides, and came up with all types of elaborate excuses as for why the puzzle pieces didn't fit. When I ran out of excuses, I did the next best thing I knew which was to try to ram the ill-fitting pieces in my flesh - conjured relationship puzzle with the hope that the deformed pieces would fit. Thankfully the Lord had enough and allowed the door to close on the relationship with me relatively unharmed. I later heard about other women who encountered this preacher but were not so fortunate. One actually was so scarred by his lies and manipulation that she had to seek professional help and counseling.

I've learned that when we are patient with God's plan for our life (especially during our singleness) that patience serves as our protection. Therefore, "Be not weary in well doing for you shall reap a harvest if you faint not." (Galatians 6:9) Satan would love to make you think that God has forgotten about you, but that is simply not true. The Lord "looks down from heaven" and sees you (Psalms 33:13). God will never miss anything concerning you.

Today, make the decision that you are going to wait on God and that you will wait for Him well; so you too can sing like the sweet songbird, Juanita Bynum, that you don't mind waiting.

Prayer

Lord, I pray that you will bless me as I make the decision to wait in faith on your promises concerning my life. You have stated in your word that those who wait on you shall mount up with wings like eagles; they shall run and not faint. They shall walk and not grow weary. (Isaiah 40:31) I believe your word to be true and ask that you strengthen, restore and refresh me in this season. I pray you will use this time in my life to prepare me for the things of you.

Teach me your ways, teach me your heart and give me your direction. When I feel anxious or when worry or doubts try to creep in, Lord, please calm my fears. I thank you for this time in my life where you are teaching me to trust you, and listen to your quiet, calm, still voice. I thank you Lord that you have called me to be like the tree planted by the water. I will produce fruit in due season. (Psalm 1:3) Until that season comes, I thank you for the strength to wait well with expectation, faith and praise in my heart.
In Jesus's name, Amen.

The Heart of God

But let patience have its perfect work, that you may be perfect and complete, lacking nothing.
James 1:4

The Lord is not slow in keeping His promise, as some understand slowness. Instead he is patient with you, not wanting anyone to perish, but everyone to come to repentance.
2 Peter 3:9

But those who wait on the Lord shall renew their strength, they shall mount up with wings like eagles, they shall run and not be weary, they shall walk and not faint.
Isaiah 40:32

CHAPTER 2

Have Faith Even When It Seems Impossible

There are some days when it seems like marriage will never happen for you. The evenings of coming home to an empty house after a long day's work, dining alone at restaurants, attending events where it seems as if everyone is coupled and having an amazing time...this endless routine provides the perfect set up for worry and dejection to enter into your life. However, God wants you to know that even in these situations -- *have faith and know that He is a God that can move in impossible circumstances.*

I remember, for so long, I thought I would be single forever. It had been an earnest prayer of mine to have a godly husband and to do God's work with a life-long partner. Yet, it seemed as if God were ignoring my requests. While He opened great doors of favor for me in ministry, and my professional career, the door that I desperately wanted open – the door of marriage appeared bolted shut. It's important to understand that Satan, the enemy, prowls around as a roaring lion, seeking whomever he can destroy (1 Peter 5:8), therefore he will use moments of hopelessness and despair to breed anxiety and weaken your faith. Perhaps you've heard some of his lies:

15

"You will never marry!"
"You're too old. No one will want you."
"You are too involved in the church, you scare men away!"

I've heard all these lies before. Yet, even in my bleakest moments, when it seemed I failed to attract the attention of *any* man, let alone a man that could be my future husband, I stood on the word of God. I would muster all my strength and yell, *"Satan, I rebuke you in the name of Jesus Christ. The Lord HAS heard my prayers for a godly husband and I believe they are coming into manifestation NOW!"*

YOU MUST SPEAK LIFE

As believers in Jesus Christ, we have power in our confession and are called to speak faith filled words. Even in times of great hardship, trials and tribulation, when it seems like nothing is happening, we are to call things "that are not as though they are." (Romans 4:17)

Despite my husband seemingly nowhere around, I countered every taunt and jeer thrown by Satan with the word of God. For every dashed hope or false start with a potential suitor (which Satan loved to bring to my remembrance), and when I couldn't think of an appropriate scripture, I simply took a deep breath, squared my shoulders and declared in the words of Prophet Rogers Decuir of Pasadena, California: *"I believe God."* Whatever lie or negative thought Satan tried to plant in my heart, I would uproot with my repetition of faith: "*I believe God. I believe God. I believe God!*"

Some of my declarations were:
I believe God is preparing me for my husband.
I believe God is preparing my husband for me.
I believe we will work together and do great work for God's glory.
I believe I will see the manifestation of every promise and good thing God has for my family, my life and me.

Your mouth holds great power, and your words serve as containers of either blessings or destruction. Despite what your situation may look like, no matter how long you've been single, your age, your financial status or the number of kids out of wedlock you may have; know that when God has a blessing for you, there is nothing Satan can do to stop it. Satan will in turn try to use you to block your own blessings by speaking death and destruction over your future, however don't fall for the bait.

If you have ever found yourself lamenting to your girlfriends or family members, "*I'll never get married.*" Or "*There just aren't any good men out here,*" Stop and repent. Ask God to fill your mouth with *His* words, and to help you only verbalize words that line up with His will for your life.

This is the time to strengthen your faith and you don't want to miss your destiny because you lacked the faith and the strength to cross the finish line. Remember: it's impossible to please God without faith (Hebrews 11:6). You need faith as a believer and you need supernatural faith to believe God for what only He can do. If you find your faith waning or feel yourself spiritually empty, dive deep in the word of God. Remember; faith comes by hearing the word of God. (Romans 10:17) Surround yourself with people, places and things where God's word is being taught and spoken.

FROM WARFARE TO VICTORY

There were many days, when I would plug scriptures into my smartphone and schedule them to pop up several times throughout the day. I would anoint myself daily before work and put on my spiritual armor (Ephesians 6:10-18). Not only did I put on my spiritual armor to fight the imps and demonic influences that presented themselves on my job, but also to guard my mind so my thoughts and heart lined up with the word of God. The fight we fight is a spiritual fight, not a natural fight, and there will be seasons during your singleness where you will have to fight for faith. So if you need more faith, ask God for it:

Ask and it shall be given to you; seek and you will find; knock and the door will be opened to you. For everyone who asks receives; the one who seeks finds; and to the one who knocks, the door will be opened. Which of you if your son asks for bread, will you give him a stone? Of if he asks for a fish, will you give him a snake? If you then, though you are evil know how to give good gifts to your children, how much more will your Father in heaven give good gifts to those who ask Him! – Matthew 7:7-9

It pleases God when we ask for glorious things such as faith. For Christians, faith serves as the foundation of who we are and what we believe. After battling so long with the devil and having different encounters where my faith was tested, I finally reached a point where Satan realized that I wasn't budging from my position-- that despite what it looked like, I believed God and believed that He would send me a godly husband. That was my position, my belief, and nothing could move me from believing otherwise. Satan ultimately realized this, and quit provoking me in this particular area. He never stopped harassing me completely during my singleness, but in the area of my faith, he learned I would not be moved.

This was only possible, because of God's grace and strength. I cried out to Him daily for renewed faith and He met and exceeded my every need. God desires to do the same for you, but first you must be willing to believe in God for your every situation, even when it seems impossible. The God we serve is a big, big God and will always come to our rescue.

Prayer

Lord, you said it is impossible for me to please you without having faith (Hebrews 11:6), therefore I ask God that you strengthen and make me steadfast in the area of my faith. I believe God that your word is true and know that if I have faith the size of a mustard seed, and then nothing is impossible for you. Help me to fight this good fight of faith concerning my desire for marriage. Help me to not lose perspective and lose sight of what you are doing in my life.

Teach and help me to cast down every thought and imagination that does not line up with your word. For I know the weapons you have given me to fight with are not the weapons of this world, but they are spiritual weapons to pull down and demolish any strongholds and falsehoods that are not of you. (2 Corinthians 10:4) Teach me to be a woman of faith who puts her complete trust in you, knowing you will strengthen me and teach me every step of the way. I praise you in advance for giving me the victory over the enemy.
In Jesus' name, Amen.

The Heart of God

He replied, "Because you have so little faith. Truly I tell you, if you have faith as small as a mustard seed, you can say to this mountain, 'Move from here to there,' and it will move. Nothing will be impossible for you.
Matthew 17:20

This is the confidence we have in approaching God: that if we ask anything according to His will, He hears us. And if we know that He hears us in whatever we ask, we know that we have the requests, which we have asked from Him.
1 John 5:14-15

Now faith is confidence in what we hope for and assurance about what we do not see.
Hebrews 11:1

CHAPTER 3

The Ache of Loneliness

As a single you will undoubtedly experience moments where you feel all alone as if God has abandoned you. I remember enduring a particular season of my singleness where I felt so lonely my heart ached. I had a wonderful family; great people at my job and church that I interacted regularly with; yet, in spite of these great people, my soul felt empty. I desired my partner, my husband, the one who would complete me and make me feel whole. It was a heartfelt crave, a cry and longing that came from the deep recess of my soul.

"God, where is my husband?" I often inquired. I thought, *"Surely if my husband were here, I wouldn't feel so lonely." "If he were here, I would have someone to eat dinner with"*, I thought. These streams of thoughts continued with suppositions and imagings such as: I would have someone to share my day with and someone to attend church with and compare notes about the service with. I had in mind that this imagined husband would be someone I could give my heart to who was trustworthy of confiding my deepest secrets and fears to.

In seeking God, I questioned, *"God, what is taking so long? I am just so lonely."*

I often felt as if my heart were breaking and, even though I felt the presence of God and knew He was with me, it seemed as if He was far away and had left me all alone, forgotten and abandoned. I would marvel at how I had come to this situation where it seemed as if I didn't have a friend in the world and how I became to feel so lonely and isolated. Then I remembered how God slowly and methodically shut the door to friendships and relationships that did not glorify Him. The process began rather innocuously after I had completed my first spiritual fast, resulting in a deeper hunger and thirst for God. The fast also broke the generational chains of alcoholism that were beginning to take root in my life. Because I no longer drank alcohol, the invitations to the after work happy hours and the bars no longer came. My friends would exclaim, "*Wow, you've changed. You're so churchy now.*"

I did my best to protest. I tried to prove that I hadn't changed, that I was still the same ole Kacie. But the truth was, I *had* changed. God had begun to change me from the inside. My appetite and taste buds were different. The gossip-laden conversations filled with profanity, the work-related political strategy sessions seeped in ego and a desire for power no longer appealed to me. I was being transformed, and in order to go to places God was taking me, I knew that, I would have to leave some things behind and some friends who were not ready to give their lives to Jesus. The connections and attachments I had to certain friends and colleagues had to be removed, otherwise, I would never reach the destination God had for me.

PURPOSE IN LONELINESS

Perhaps, you find yourself single and alone too. Whatever the circumstances that led to this point, understand that this is all part of God's plan to mold and shape you into the woman you need to be. I will freely admit that loneliness can hurt. But, if you stay with me in this chapter, I will demonstrate how you can endure this season and emerge strengthened and firmly planted for God's glory.

The purpose of my journey in singleness and enduring such extreme feelings of loneliness was to learn foremost that God was with me and would never leave or forsake me. I had to learn by experience that when I didn't have a friend to go shopping, or a girlfriend to chat with on the phone, I had the Lord. I discovered that I could call Him up and talk about anything that was on my mind. It was now so simple. I was reared in the church, and heard all the popular clichés about God being an "on time God" and available whenever needed. However, it took me having no one else in my life to turn to for me to finally realize that God truly was always available. With God, I was not alone, and I could talk to Him whenever I needed.

BATTLING LONELINESS

That's exactly what I did- when I felt lonely, I talked to God. When I felt abandoned, I shared my concerns with him. When I felt misunderstood and rejected by people, I cried out to Him. Prior to this revelation, I had filled my life's empty spaces with people, food or sex; but this time God was doing something new in me. He was using my singleness to teach me how to turn to Him and get filled by His Spirit. His methodology presented a permanent solution to my situation, where my past remedies were only haphazard and temporary stop - gaps.

This is the wonderful way God can work in our lives if we allow Him. I previously thought that if I surrounded myself with more people, excelled further in my career, or even ate the most delectable foods, the empty places in my life would be filled. For such a long time, I believed that my loneliness would even be eradicated boy a husband; that if God blessed me with a husband, my life would be better, I would have a spouse and therefore wouldn't be so lonely. But, God used my loneliness and isolation season to purify, and teach me that He was *all* I needed. He brought me to a point where I could accept in my heart, whether or not God blessed me with a husband, as long as I had God, He was all I needed.

Once this was settled in my heart, I pursued Him even more deeply. There were days when I still felt lonely. However I was determined to allow God to heal me and make me whole. Instead of eating out, I dined with Jesus at my home. I would light candles, play gospel music and enjoy dinner with Jesus. I meditated and constantly studied the word of God. Prior to this, I had been so busy with other things, that I had never taken the time to truly learn the word of God. (Much of my biblical knowledge was from what I learned while attending a Christian elementary school.) Therefore, being an adult, my knowledge of scripture was limited and underdeveloped.

I needed to overcome this and asked God for a great hunger for and an understanding of His word. Each day after work, I would come home and watch pre-recorded messages from my favorite televangelists. Powerful teachings by Bishop T.D. Jakes, Joyce Meyer and Joel Osteen helped sustain me and develop me during this time. I also became more involved in my church, leading my first Sunday school session and created a new Facebook account, called Inspired Overflow that is now used to bless and encourage the world through the inspired messages of God. It took God removing the people and distractions from my life in order for me to realize that it was necessary for me to be lonely during this season. I had become too distracted and focused on things that were unrelated to God, and I needed a break from all distractions. I needed a time of solitude where it was just God and I so I could learn and appreciate His soft, still voice.

Even though the feelings of loneliness never completely subsided, the aching of loneliness did. As I dived deeper into having a true relationship with the Lord, I accepted His will for my life, including a willingness to endure my season of loneliness. After accepting this time as God's will, He gave me the grace and the strength to endure.

GOD IS WITH YOU

My dear sister, God wants you to know that He sees you and has not forgotten about you. Jeremiah 31:3 says *"God draws us with his loving kindness."* If you are feeling lonely as if God has forgotten you, "lift up your eyes to the mountains" because that is where your help comes from. (Psalm 121:1) From heaven, the Lord extends His hand to you to inform you that He hasn't forgotten nor will he ever forget about you. If you feel that Satan is working overdrive in the area of loneliness to attack you make sure you counter him with the word of God.

Remember, that God sent His only son Jesus to die on the cross for you and He loves you very much. As He willingly sacrificed His son Jesus for your eternal life, you can believe that He will never ever leave or abandon you. God sees and walks beside you every step of the way. Do not run from this special time of your life. Embrace this anointed season where it's just you and the Father. In the end, you'll be glad you did.

Prayer

Dear God,

Help me to always understand that you are with me each and every step of the way, even during the moments when I feel so alone. Help me to not get caught up in my emotions, but in your truth where you said you would never leave me or forsake me (Hebrews 13:5) Just as you commanded Joshua to be strong and courageous through your grace, I will be strong in this season. For I know you are with me always (Matthew 28:20). Finally Lord, you have promised that no matter what I go through, I am never alone. Use this time in my life to mold me into the woman you have called me to be. Develop my ears so I never miss your voice, and comfort my heart so I know you are always near.

In Jesus' name, Amen.

The Heart of God

Teaching them to observe all that I commanded you; and lo, I am with you always, even to the end of the age.
Matthew 28:20

A father of the fatherless and a judge for the widows is God in His holy habitation. God makes a home for the lonely; He leads out the prisoners into prosperity, only the rebellious dwell in the parched land.
Psalm 68:5-6

Can a woman forget her nursing child and have no compassion on the son of her womb? Even these may forget, but I will not forget you.
Isaiah 49:15

"For I know the plans I have for you," declares the Lord, "plans to prosper you and not to harm you, plans to give you hope and a future."
Jeremiah 29:11

CHAPTER 4

Be Saved and Sanctified for God's Great Work

God desires to use your singleness as a time to draw you closer to Him. In order for this to happen there are some things regarding your lifestyle and thought patterns that must change until they conform to Christ's mindset. As a single woman, I needed a complete shift in the way I thought. For so long I had looked at singleness through the perspective of the world, which blinded me to the pitfalls and trappings, found in the world's singleness.

Singleness as presented by Carrie Bradshaw along with her girlfriends Samantha, Charlotte and Miranda from TV's Sex in the City made being single appear sexy, flirty and fun. My escapades however weren't nearly as fun. They were filled with drama as I often rebounded quickly from long-term relationship to long-term relationship with quick intervals of singleness in between. My momentary moments of singleness were like pit stops. I stayed single long enough to change my hairstyle, buy new makeup and then *whoosh* --- I was back out in the rat race. I never took the time to assess where I was emotionally or mentally, let alone spiritually. In fact, my spiritual recovery and health were the last things I was concerned about.

BLESSINGS OF SUBMISSION

It took God arresting my spirit one evening when I finally decided once and for all that I was willing to completely surrender my entire life (including my single status) to Him. After enjoying a family outing during a hot summer night, I returned home to my cool apartment and felt a strong desire to pray. The feeling was so urgent that I could hardly get my key into the door. I didn't know what was happening. In fact, all I knew was that there was an enormous pull upon my spirit calling me to surrender to God's will for my life.

The pull was so great and the force was so strong that all I could do was cry, "Yes!" to God. I began to pray over my life. I knew God was calling me deeper to Him, and yet all I could say was, "Yes, God yes!" Back then I didn't know what Jesus was calling me into, but I knew that it could only begin with my "Yes" to Him.

This call on my life occurred during a time when I was undistracted by a relationship. (Had I been involved in a relationship during this time when I felt the enormous pull upon my spirit by God, it could have been very likely that I would have missed this moment. I would have returned to my apartment ready to go out for a drink or to dinner; instead of realizing the need to pray.) God instead used my singleness to arrest my heart and hear His voice.

Too often we try to rush our season of singleness and consume ourselves with busyness and we miss the voice of God. I was at a point where I needed to hear from God, and needed a divine intervention in my life. I was very successful in my professional career, but behind closed doors my life was a wreck. I was drinking heavily, relieving my night, I finished as I applied my makeup and listened to music the next morning on my way to work. My alcohol consumption fueled poor decision-making and opened the door to lust and perversion in my life. I even entered a torrid love affair with a man who openly renounced and opposed God. My life was spinning out of control.

LIVE FOR GOD

As the Holy Spirit tugged on my heart that summer night in my apartment, I was presented with a choice: either I could choose to submit to God's will for my life, or I could follow the path I was currently on leading to death and destruction. I chose that night to follow God. At the time, I wasn't sure what it all meant, but there was something on the inside of me that kept screaming, *"Yes!"* to God's plan.

Perhaps you find yourself in an unfamiliar state. The old way of doing things no longer works for you. Perhaps through this book, or words spoken to you at church or by loved ones; you find yourself desiring something different for your life. The tugging you feel at your spirit is God seeking your attention.

He's wooing you. As Christians we all have a choice on how we will walk during the journey of life.

Deuteronomy 30:19 refers to our decisions as a choice between "life and death," instructing us to "choose life." The evening when I decided to say yes to God, I made the decision to choose life and live for God. I traded in my secret uniform from the devil and went fully on the Lord's team. In return, the Lord filled me that night with His Holy Spirit with the evidence of speaking in tongues. Glory hallelujah!

After making the decision to choose life and become set apart for God's glory, God began to work on my mind and heart. Through the prompting of the Holy Spirit, I immediately made the decision to no longer engage in pre-marital sex and that I would wait for God to bring my husband. Regardless of how long I would have to wait, I was going to trust God to bring me my husband at His appointed time. I was adamant in my decision and stood boldly. The next time I had sex would be with my husband on our wedding night.

No longer would I entertain drunken escapades with married men or interested admirers. I would no longer defile my body or allow it to be defiled by others. I was God's girl. His daughter, His special jewel and as He cleaned and dusted me off, no man's fingertips would touch me sexually until we entered into Holy matrimony. In order to remain steadfast in my decision, I knew

I needed to be rooted in God's word. I studied scriptures on sanctification and learned the importance of being transformed and renewed in my mind. Scriptures such as 1 Peter 1:16 jumped out at me:

"You shall be holy, for I am holy."

Others like, 1 Peter 2:9 reinforced what I heard the Holy Spirit speaking. That I was important, that I was special to Him, *His royal priesthood and special possession*, and that I was truly on the right track in respecting my body and keeping it holy and pure for God's glory. During your time of singleness, make sure you become rooted in God's word and learn to meditate on scripture. Oftentimes the world will fool you and make you think certain acts and lifestyles are okay, partly because they are so commonplace on the radio or on television. However, adhere to the word of God.

For a period of time, the enemy made me feel like it would be impossible to abstain from sex. He even tried to convince me that if I refrained from having sex by waiting on my husband I would somehow 'forget' how to do 'it' or my technique would be outdated and out of style. (As a married woman who successfully remained celibate until marriage I can assure you that I have not missed a beat!) Satan is a deceiver and will do everything He can to prevent you from reaching your destiny, even if that means conjuring up lies that speak to your deepest and darkest fears.

When it comes to fornication, which is sex outside of marriage, this is an area of grave danger; do not fool around with it. If you are having sex and are not married, please stop now (even if you are widowed, divorced, over the age of 50....if you are unmarried and having sex stop now from committing this sin.) The Lord will give you strength to overcome in this area. I admonish you to pray and ask God to deliver you from fornication. Fornication is dangerous and is regarded as an umbrella sin --- it's a type of sin that opens the door to other accompanying sins. All Satan needs is an entry to come wreak havoc in your life.

When you engage in fornication you commit a sin against your body. In other words, you create hurt, harm and damage to yourself. If you find yourself believing the lie from Satan that it is impossible for you to resist sex, know that the God you serve is mighty and powerful and He gives you everything you need to resist the enemy. In fact, 1 Corinthians 10:13 says that God always "makes a way of escape for us when presented with temptation." We must simply be obedient and do what the word says, which instructs us to "flee from fornication." (1 Corinthians 6:18)

FREEDOM

Through His resurrection power, Jesus has overcome the world and Satan's efforts cannot harm or overtake us. (John 16:33). Satan will fight and do everything he can to keep you in the traps of sin. However, be encouraged, because the God we serve is more powerful and has given us the victory. Once I made the decision to no longer engage in fornication, and to be sanctified and set apart for God's glory, I needed the supernatural power that could only come through prayer and fasting to strengthen and encourage me on my journey. There had been years of fornication and sexual sin built up in my life that resulted in layers upon layers that needed to be sloughed from my spirit. Fasting and prayer helped destroy the old mindsets that had established themselves as strongholds in my life.

John 8:38 says "Whom the Son of God has set free is free indeed." I confessed my freedom from my past, and warred in the spirit through prayer and meditating on the Word to be delivered and set free.

There was one particular soul tie that seemed impossible to break -- the soul tie I had with an unbeliever. What once began as romantic and exciting ended as spiritually violent and demonic. For the life of me, I couldn't let go of this particular relationship in my heart. I confessed scriptures, I meditated on the Word, I prayed and asked God to free me, but deep in my heart, I cared for this person and longed for his friendship and companionship.

After being saved and filled with the Holy Ghost, I followed God's instruction and immediately severed the ties with the individual; however, my heart still ached. I detested feeling this way for a man that was not my husband, and who was open about his lack of belief in God, however I couldn't seem to break the connection. He wasn't good for me. He did not mean me any good; yet, I couldn't seem to break free. One Sunday at church, I cried out to God. I wanted to be free from this man yet no matter what I seemed to do, I just couldn't get free.

The Lord showed me a vision of shackles and chains cuffed around my ankles. The enemy had me bound and refused to release me. When we engage in fornication we are literally giving Satan legal rights to our bodies. I had to war in the spirit for a very long time through much prayer and fasting to finally break free from this particular soul tie. It was hard work spiritually and a tough fight.

Satan did not let up without a fight because he knew that if I stayed in bondage I would never be able to walk fully in my purpose and anointing. Also, had I stayed bound, I would not have the testimony that I now have to share with others. There *is* power through Jesus Christ and He can break every demonic chain and stronghold in your life.

Just as you desire to live your singleness saved and set-apart for God's great work, be prepared for opposition by the enemy. Nevertheless, know that Satan's opposition is no match for the resurrecting power of Jesus Christ! The process of being sanctified and set-apart for God's glory is just that – a process. It is a journey that begins with a decision that you will choose life and submit to God's plan. God desires to use you to advance His kingdom and must do so through a vessel that is clean, pure and untainted with sin. I am a living witness that God can clean, restore and redeem you to do His great work regardless of your past.

When you follow the urging of the Apostle Paul to present yourself as a "living sacrifice that is holy and acceptable to God," then you really are living your life unto worship to Him (God). (Romans 12:1) Today, make the decision that you will worship God with your body and that you will be a saved, sanctified and a set-apart single woman, until God presents you to the worthy man that He ordains as your husband.

Prayer

Dear God,

I thank you for coming into my life and for saving me--- because of your ultimate sacrifice, you came into this world so I may have life and live it abundantly. (John 10:10) I now ask you God to help refine and mature me in you. I know that to have an abundant life, there are some things I must let go from my past. I seek your Holy Spirit to purify me and deliver me. Mold me into the woman you have designed me to be. Touch my heart and my mind.

I desire to be set apart for your glory. Renew my mind in the things of you. Give me your mindset concerning my relationships, my spiritual walk and my life for you. Anoint me as your daughter. I submit my life to you and thank you knowing that as mold and shape me; you are with me every step of the way.
In Jesus' name,
Amen.

The Heart of God

They are not of the world just as I am not of the world.
Sanctify them in the truth; your word is the truth.
John 17:16-17

I appeal to you therefore, brothers, by the mercies of God, to
present your bodies as a living sacrifice, holy and acceptable to
God, which is your spiritual worship.
Romans 12:1

But put on the Lord Jesus Christ and make no provision for
the flesh, to gratify its desires.
Romans 13:14

Therefore, if anyone is in Christ, he is a new creation. The old
has passed away; behold, the new has come.
2 Corinthians 5:17

CHAPTER 5

Avoid Satan's Counterfeits

B e on the lookout for Satan's counterfeits that will come into your life posing as the real thing. During my singlehood I encountered a true counterfeit, that had I not been under the covering of God, I would have fallen victim to his wiles and deceit. As you pray to God for your husband, make sure you remain sober, vigilant and alert. (1 Peter 5:7) When Jesus sent His disciples to proclaim His word, He informed them that He was sending them out as "sheep amongst wolves" and because of this they should be "wise as serpents and harmless as doves." (Matthew 10:16) Because you desire a godly marriage and want nothing more than to live your current singleness in a way that is honorable and pleasing to God, Satan would love to trip you up with one of his counterfeits – a man presenting himself as the one sent by God but in reality is the exact opposite.

I have a favorite summer fragrance that I love to wear. The scent is light, fresh and reminds me of a crisp, clean sky right after a summer rain. This perfume makes me happy; and whenever I wear it, someone always comments on how wonderful the fragrance smells. The only issue I have with this fragrance is the cost -- it's expensive. A tiny bottle costs a fortune, so one day while out on my lunch break, I pulled into a strip mall to buy a sandwich from my favorite lunch shop, and was approached by a man selling items from his car trunk.

His trunk contained everything: designer purses, socks, hats, costume jewelry and...My favorite perfume! I didn't think or care how this man had come to acquire all these things or why he was selling them from the trunk of his car, all I knew was that he had my *favorite* perfume and was willing to sell me a full sized bottle for a very cheap price.

I happily completed my purchase with the man selling items from his trunk and ignored the nagging feeling forming in my gut. This was *my* lucky day, I thought. I was able to enjoy my favorite sub sandwich for lunch plus purchase an enormous bottle of my favorite perfume for cheap!! It wasn't until the next day that I realized my cheap and easy perfume purchase came with consequences. Despite the packaging for the perfume being perfectly intact, one whiff of the fragrance let me know that the fragrance was a counterfeit. The light and airy scent I was familiar with was replaced with a loud and sour antiseptic smell.

"You smell like a hospital and bacon," a male friend complained. His comment solidified that I had been duped and not only was it apparent to me but obvious to others. The point I am trying to make with this story is that there are times during your

singleness where you may get tired of waiting and become tempted to compromise or settle for the counterfeit instead of the real thing.

BEWARE OF COUNTERFEITS

Counterfeits look like the original. They appear to possess the same packaging, and same label. However upon closer inspection, they never pass the smell test. Something just doesn't line up right. Jesus warned His disciples to be aware of the false prophets that went about in sheep's clothing yet on the inside were like ravenous wolves.

Jesus further instructed the disciples to look at their fruit then they would recognize those who had been sent by Him. (Matthew 7:16) Jesus' advice to His disciples rings true for today. Had I been looking at the fruit, I would have seen the telltale signs that something was awry with the perfume. I would have heeded the nagging feeling in my belly regarding the car trunk salesman and begun to think. *Who was this guy? And why was he selling items out of his trunk? Wasn't it against city ordinance to sell wares without a license? After all reputable businesses with reputable products didn't need to hawk or barter on commercial parking lots.* I should have known better, but I disregarded all the signs of a counterfeit, because I wanted the perfume and I wanted it – cheap, fast and easy.

The mindset of receiving things: cheap, fast and easy is dangerous and runs counter to having the mindset of Christ. When we have the mindset of Christ we are encouraged to use discretion, wisdom and seek His guidance for decision-making. As a single you must not allow your desire for marriage to rush you into a relationship with a counterfeit simply because you have grown tired and weary from waiting.

As you pray and spend time with God you learn to hear and discern God's voice. In John 10:27 it says, "My sheep know my voice," so when impatience begins to rise, and that attractive man is winking and grinning at you, you can catch your breath, exhale and listen to God's direction on whether or not this is the godly man sent to you.

God knows every prayer you have made concerning your desire for a husband; therefore it is impossible to mess up, lose or cancel what God has for you, regardless of the length of time you have been waiting. Satan, the father of all lies, has absolutely no authority over what God has designated for your life, so refuse to listen to Him, especially when he taunts you for refusing to settle and accept his counterfeit.

As God's special daughter, He has a husband that He has fashioned in His image to complement and meld with you. God knows the plans and the future He has for you both, which is why it is necessary that you become yoked with His original and not a counterfeit.

46

Ephesians 6:11 instructs us to put on the full armor of God, so that we will be able to stand firm against the schemes of the devil. Counterfeits don't always emerge from the back of car trunks or in parking lots; in fact, they can be positioned in the altar of a church. Satan tried to deceive me several times during my single, but it was the grace of God that protected me from falling into his traps.

DECEPTION

There was a young Pastor in my hometown that used Facebook to express his interest in getting to know me further. This young Pastor was articulate, good looking and appeared to embody all the qualities I had prayed to God for in a husband.

"God is HE the ONE?" I wondered.

I was flattered, excited and nervous at the level of interest with which this young Pastor pursued me. He was complimentary, respectful and he came from a solid and respected church in my hometown. I was impressed with his educational background, and his delivery of the word via his sermons posted on the web. I had desired a godly man in my life, and here God had blessed me with a pastor, who was interested in me! *"Wow, God REALLY did answer prayers"*, I marveled.

The young pastor and I began to I communicate long-distance for several months. He had recently become Pastor of a church a several hours away, and during my prayer time, I regularly asked God if this was the man that He was sending to me. I went further in prayer and asked God to show me any hidden things that I couldn't see through my natural eyes.

In prayer, God one day showed me an image of the young Pastor straining for a high goal on top of a mountain. In order for him to reach the top goal situated on the mountain, in the vision, he began to climb on my neck to reach the pinnacle. I was confused by this vision. What was God trying to show me? The Lord revealed that the young preacher wasn't interested in me, but was mainly interested in being connected to me due to the elected office I held in my hometown. Over time, the Lord revealed more and more bits and pieces that chipped away the novelty and glamour of being in a relationship with the young pastor.

Sensitive topics that I had privately confided to him regarding local politics had made its way through the grapevine of local pastors back to me. It was obvious; he could not be trusted with confidential information. Also, most glaringly, he did not share the same regard for scripture and was hesitant to support me in my decision to remain abstinent in our relationship.

I never heard an audible voice from God that the young pastor was not *"the one"* even though I really wanted to know. I believe God decided that He didn't have to speak in audible voice because He instead demonstrated that the fruit on the young pastor's spiritual tree was not good enough to eat; it was immature and contaminated. And as if I needed further proof, a well-respected pastor met me for coffee to speak about a work-related issue and very gingerly advised me to be careful in my dealings with the young pastor. He had heard through the grapevine that this young pastor and I were dating, and he had some concerns pertaining to the young pastor's reputation. My dear sister, you may not always hear the audible voice of God concerning if a relationship is right for you, but He will *speak* to you in a variety ways if you are willing to listen. Inspect the fruit on the tree of your potential mate and look for the tell tale signs.

2 Corinthians 11:14 refers to Satan disguising himself as an angel of light. The young pastor met many of the qualifications on my personal checklist on what I was looking for in a husband. However, the Lord knew better and refused to allow me to get confused or tangled with one of the enemy's counterfeits. The Lord will protect you if you heed and listen to His direction, which is what I did. I broke off the relationship with the young pastor -- much to his surprise.

Be sure to listen to God and obey Him, even when He tells you no. God knows best and He can see beyond what your natural eyes can see. God also knows the hearts of men and can see the hidden motives and ambitions behind the smooth speech and articulate tongue. This is not the time to settle for Satan's counterfeits. There is too much at stake. Your future and your destiny depend on you being yoked with the true man of God that has been ordained for you. Wait on God with prayer, vigilance and discernment. God is with you and will show you exactly what you need to see in order for you to recognize God's best.

Prayer

Dear God,

Open my eyes so I can see what you have for me by recognizing your best. Unplug my ears so I will listen to your still, quiet voice. Help me to seek you in all things and not be distracted or lose focus through the plans of Satan. I thank you for stirring the gift of discernment inside me. I thank you for showing every hidden motive of others concerning me, and for protecting me from Satan's counterfeits which attempt to keep me from receiving your best. I accept your best. I receive the best you have for my life, and I wait on you with faithful expectation. In Jesus' name, Amen.

The Heart of God

But the Lord said to Samuel, "Do not look at his appearance
or at the height of his stature, because I have rejected him;
for God sees not as man sees for man looks at the outward
appearance, but the Lord looks at the heart."
I Samuel 16:7

But I am afraid that, as the serpent deceived Eve by his
craftiness, your minds will be led astray from the simplicity
and purity of devotion to Christ.
2 Corinthians 11:3

Put on the full armor of God, so that you will be able to stand
firm against the schemes of the devil.
Ephesians 6:11

But the Lord is faithful, and He will strengthen and protect
you from the evil one.
2 Thessalonians 3:3

CHAPTER 6

Learn Contentment

For a long time I thought my good deeds would hasten God to bring a husband into my life. I mean, I was *finally* living right. I no longer attended church out of habit or tradition instead I faithfully attended because I *needed* the living word of God. I taught a Sunday school series, volunteered with local ministries and fasted and prayed regularly, therefore I couldn't understand what was taking God so long in sending me my husband.

"God, *where is my husband?!*" I would whine.

I thought since I was finally doing things God should bring me my husband immediately as my reward. After all, what could possibly be taking so long? God had the power to do anything, why was He making me wait? I didn't like being single, I wanted a husband -- more specifically, I wanted a *godly husband* to do ministry work. I often wondered if God understood. Didn't He know the desires of my heart? And if He did, what on earth was taking so long?

A HEART TEST

I felt I was ready for marriage. However, God knew better. Even though I was actively serving in my church, highlighting scriptures in my Bible and confessing the word of God over my life, my heart still needed repair. God used my time of singleness to test my heart and my motives, while also teaching me the importance of contentment. Proverbs 16:2 says, *"All a person's ways seem pure to them, but motives are weighed by the Lord."* God wants to ensure that your motives for serving Him are pure and centered on Him. I loved the Lord and I loved serving Him, but if I am honest with myself, I realize my motives were not always pure. I felt that if I served God faithfully then He should and would reward me with a husband.

Much akin to my professional career in politics, I expected quid pro quo or a fair exchange for goods with my relationship with God. If I did "X" for God then I expected Him to do "Y" for me. After all, wasn't that fair? Over time, I had to learn that God was not a genie in a bottle, manipulated by my will, wants and emotions. He instead was a sovereign God who moved when He wanted to move, and it was my responsibility to trust Him and be content whether I remained single or married.

THE JOURNEY TO CONTENTMENT

In the letter to the Christian church in the city of Philippi, the Apostle Paul writes *"I know what it is to be in need, and I know what it is to have plenty. I have learned the secret of being content in any and every situation."* (Philippians 4:12) The definition of contentment is "being satisfied with whatever you have." The Apostle Paul is a great example of an individual who decided through experience that whether he had much or had little, he made the decision that he would be content.

As a single woman, I believe God wants you to have this same attitude and to stress the point, He will allow you to go through multiple tests to ensure this important spiritual principle dwells in your heart. For so long, I fought the spirit of contentment. I didn't want to be content as a single! I wanted a husband; and the idea of embracing contentment seemed too passive and laid back for my urgent desire and quest for marriage.

I cared about meeting a godly man and getting married much more than I cared or valued learning how to be grateful and satisfied with whatever state God had placed me. The Lord began to show me that my desire for a husband had become an idol in my life, and that I would never marry until I made the decision to marry Him first. He began to show me the Apostle Paul's words concerning contentment, and instead of scrunching my face, whining and complaining, I asked God to guide and teach me how, I too, could learn the secret of contentment.

I had spent so much time praying about *not* being single that I needed to overhaul my prayer requests. My priorities began to shift as my heart began to settle on the idea that if God never sent me a husband, He was still worthy to be praised. I began to ask God to teach me how to be faithful in serving Him and content as a single woman. I meditated on Philippians 4:12 regularly. When scrolling through Facebook and bombarded with announcements of friends' engagements and weddings, I prayed for my contentment. During the holidays when it seemed everyone had someone, and I found myself alone; I prayed for contentment. When I came home to an empty house after a long day's work, without anyone to talk with or share my day, I prayed to God for soul-satisfying contentment.

Becoming content in where God has you is important because it thwarts Satan's ability to distract and lure you away from God. In the past, I would see other women blessed with their boyfriends and fiancés, knowing they were co-habitating and fornicating. The enemy would remind me of their lifestyles to have me bitter or resentful towards God. *See how they are blessed? They lived together, had sex and now are married. You on the other hand are still lonely and single.* As I learned to be content, I was able to rebuke Satan and simply reply with, *"That's not my business!"* and I would pray for peace and genuine happiness for the woman that was being blessed with marriage.

THE SECRET

In the text, Apostle Paul writes that he has "learned the secret of contentment." I prayed and asked God to give me the secret, because I desperately needed it. I wanted to feel content and secure with where God had me. I believe God wants us all to know the secret, so I will share what God told me: The secret in contentment is knowing that it's God who orchestrates our steps; and because God is the one who orchestrates our steps, we can rest fully assured knowing He has us exactly where we need to be. He is not withholding anything good from us. He uses every situation to strengthen and draw us near to Him. I believe when you truly understand that the will of God for your life is always good, you can rest at ease, knowing that whatever state you are in, it is necessary and it is truly for your good.

CHOOSE CONTENTMENT

I know my desire for marriage was a godly desire. I believe God wants to grant marriage to those who desire marriage. Psalm 84:11 says *"God will not withhold any good thing from those who walk uprightly in Him."* The desire and earnestness I had for marriage was not a bad thing. The idol that I had made regarding marriage and my lack of contentment and willingness to submit to God's plan and timetable *was* a bad thing. Contentment is a pre-determined mindset.

Through the grace and power of God, you can be content as a Christian single. There were many days that I had to liken the spirit of contentment as to putting on a pair of jeans daily. I would tell myself, *"Today, I choose to be content."* I choose to trust God's plan and timetable for my life. For the days when contentment just seems too hard to bear, take comfort in the Apostle Paul's writing, where he cites his source for strength. *"I can do all things through Christ who strengthens me."* (Philippians 4:13)

The Apostle Paul knew that He didn't have to do the work of being content alone. He knew that through the power of Jesus Christ, He would give him everything He needed. The same holds true for you today. Trust Jesus to give you the strength and discipline you need, to be content so you can enjoy right where you are.

Prayer

Dear God,

Teach me to be content in every aspect of my life. Even when I don't understand, help me to trust you in everything. Lord, touch my mind where I don't lose focus and become distracted by what others have. Let me be satisfied with just you, your presence and your spirit. Let that be enough for me. I acknowledge you as the head of my life. I trust that everything you do is for my good.

I thank you for blessing me with the spirit of peace and removing any anger or bitterness from my soul. I ask for forgiveness for the times when I refused to accept your will and became angry. This day forward, I choose to embrace being content in whatever state you have me in, knowing that in all things it is for your ultimate glory.

In Jesus' name. Amen

The Heart of God

I know what it is to be in need, and I know what it is to have plenty. I have learned the secret of being content in any and every situation whether well fed or hungry, whether living in plenty or in want.
Philippians 4:12

Keep your lives free from the love of money and be content with what you have, because God has said, "Never will I leave you; never will I forsake you."
Hebrews 13:5

You will keep him in perfect peace whose mind is stayed on you because he trusts in you.
Isaiah 26:3

CHAPTER 7

A Guide to Fasting

In other sections of this book I have mentioned the power that derives from the spiritual discipline of fasting and prayer. It was prayer and fasting that delivered me from a lifestyle of heavy drinking and sex. This included pornography and lust that dominated my singleness. Fasting and prayer are spiritual disciplines that I have learned to continually incorporate in my spiritual walk to ensure I remain connected and intimate with our Heavenly Father.

It was through fasting that I learned to develop a spiritual ear to hear God's voice and gain the ability to write this book. The purpose of this chapter is to encourage you to begin incorporating fasting and prayer into your spiritual life if you haven't already, and if you have, continue to fast, pray and seek greater intimacy with God throughout your singleness and as a married woman.

WHY FAST?

I grew up in a church that rarely talked about fasting. In fact it wasn't until my early 30's that I participated in my first spiritual fast; this fast forever changed my life. Fasting is mentioned both in the Old and New Testaments as an expected spiritual discipline for all believers. Bible greats such as Moses, Esther and even Jesus practiced fasting. In fact, in Matthew 6:16, Jesus begins a conversation with His disciples using the words, *"When you fast."* Jesus doesn't use the words "if" or "perhaps" but instead says *"When you fast"* indicating this is an expected practice to be adhered to by His followers.

I have witnessed fasting to be a wonderful way to inspect my heart and motives. It is a wonderful way to place God front and center in your life by allowing your natural desires to take a back seat to gain greater intimacy with the Lord. Fasting allows your prayer life to become strengthened, because your time, attention and focus are on the Lord. I liken fasting to spiritual weight lifting - as you fast and pray, your spiritual muscles develop.

When fasting, your ability to hear God becomes clearer as you use this time of consecration to seek Him and grow spiritually. If you desire greater insight, revelation an intimacy with the Lord, then fasting and prayer is your solution. Fasting is also a wonderful opportunity to intercede and ask God for His divine intervention in times of trouble. Bible heroes such as Esther and King Jehoshaphat petitioned God for intervention and protection from their enemies through fasting and prayer.

HOW TO FAST

There are many different ways to fast, and I believe it's important to not get sidetracked with the type of fast you choose; instead focus on being sure you have been called by God to begin a fast. I have completed several different types of fast during my Christian walk. Examples include: an Absolute Fast, where I have had no food for a specific number of days, a Partial Fast where I have abstained from food for 12 hours each day, a Juice Fast where I have only consumed juices and water and a Drought Fast where I have abstained from all TV, radio and social media.

Regardless of the fast I have chosen, I always made sure it was with the right intention and not to "fast just to fast" out of habit or religion. Many times before a fast, I will write a petition or a list of things I am directly seeking from God during my fast.

With my first fast, which was a 30 day partial fast, I excitedly wrote a long detailed list of my prayer requests. Many items on my petition list dealt with areas I desired God to move concerning my spiritual walk. I wanted to grow closer to God, to learn how to hear His voice, and understand scripture better. I also desired a husband and wanted to stop drinking so much alcohol as my consumption was getting out hand.

Many of the items on my list eventually came to pass; they manifested slowly with the exception of one request – and that was the one regarding my alcohol consumption. Much of my social and professional life revolved around drinking. I had a bottle of wine always uncorked at my office. During Christmas many lobbyists would provide elected officials with a bottle of wine as a gift, so I kept the bottles stashed in my office. It wasn't uncommon for me to have a drink on Friday mornings as a salute to the approaching weekend, nor was it uncommon for me to drink during the lunch hour with my afternoon meal.

My life was spiraling downward because of the alcohol; I had seen its unfortunate effects throughout many members in my family, despite knowing these things I was not ready to *completely* give up drinking. My fasting prayer was that I would not drink "so much." Thankfully, God ignored this request for a partial deliverance, and at the end of the 30-day fast, my appetite for alcohol was completely obliterated. In fact, when I even tried to drink alcohol I would become very sick and nauseous. God knew exactly what I needed and removed this area of bondage from my life. Praise be to God, I haven't had a drink since August 2011. Glory hallelujah!

PREPARATION

Regardless of what type of fast you choose, you want to ensure you are prepared for success. Make sure you have the right food, juice and vitamins at home prior to your fast. If you are doing an absolute fast where you will not eat or drink, consult with your doctor first. If you are pregnant, nursing or on medication, you should consider other ways to fast that won't disrupt or harm your body. Whenever I begin a fast that will run at least a few days, I always try to clear my calendar and avoid loading my schedule with unnecessary meetings and errands. I use the days prior to journal and meditate on what I am expecting and believing God for during the fast. I ensure that I always have a purpose for each fast.

Remember fasting is not a diet. Instead it is a time to focus and center on God. To avoid having your fast becoming a diet or a religious routine experience, be sure to schedule time with God. To help with this, I usually pray or read my Bible during the times I would normally eat breakfast, lunch or dinner. I have found this helps to center me and remind me of why I am fasting in the first place thus preventing the fast from becoming about weight loss or just a time when I am not eating.

During your fast, you will feel hungry and maybe even weak, when you are feeling this way, offer God the sacrifice of praise and worship. Dive in deeper and read God's word and soak in His presence. Remember, at your weakest moments, this is when God is able to come in with His strength. (2 Corinthians 12:10) I remember once while fasting, bursting into tears in my office cubicle after talking to a supervisor while working a summer job. I don't remember what exactly what was said, but I know it was something I would have normally shrugged off or even ignored had I not been fasting. But this time a wave of emotions hit me and I couldn't contain my tears. I was angry, upset and emotional.

I believe these were emotions that God was purging so my body could become cleansed of anger, irritability and bitterness. While you are fasting, Satan knows you are fasting. Furthermore, because Satan is the roaring lion always on the constant prowl, he will look for ways to disturb you and make you upset. Nevertheless, know through fasting and prayer you have the victory!

DON'T FORGET TO PRAY

As you fast, remember to pray not just for yourself, but also for your loved ones. Stand in the gap and intercede for your church and community. To this day, I continue to fast for my family members who are unsaved and for those who are saved but are yet not living completely for Jesus. As you begin a lifestyle of fasting and prayer, do not be discouraged if you do not witness immediate results. With the exception of being delivered from drinking alcohol, many of the items on my fasting petition list have manifested gradually over time.

Fasting is about building a relationship with God and growing more intimate with Him. It's a process and a journey, which is why it should be incorporated as part of every Christian believer's lifestyle. The power of fasting and prayer strengthened me as a single; it kept me disciplined, sharp and connected to God during a season filled with many twists and turns.

God desires for you to have greater intimacy with Him before you pursue marriage and intimacy with a husband. If you haven't sought God through prayer and fasting, I pray this chapter encourages you to seek Him through this very special and powerful discipline. I know your life will be blessed and forever changed.

Prayer

Dear God,

My desire is to truly have an intimate relationship with you. More than anything I want to grow in you. Teach me how to fast and hear your voice. God, grant me the desire and grace to practice this important spiritual discipline. Touch my heart and give me the right motives for fasting and prayer. Lord, I desire to grow and mature in you. Direct my ways and develop my path, as I grow closer to you. Move in my life in a way like never before.

In Jesus' name. Amen.

The Heart of God

"But this kind does not go out except by prayer and fasting."
Matthew 17:21

Go, gather together all the Jews who are in Susa, and fast for me. Do not eat or drink for three days, night or day. I and my attendants will fast as you do. When this is done, I will go to the king, even though it is against the law. And if I perish, I perish.
Esther 4:16

Jesus answered, "It is written: 'Man shall not live on bread alone, but by every word that comes from the mouth of God."
Matthew 4:4

"Is not this the kind of fasting I have chosen: to loose the chains of injustice and untie the cords of the yoke, to set the oppressed free and break every yoke?
Isaiah 58:6

Alarmed, Jehoshaphat resolved to inquire of the Lord, and he proclaimed a fast for all Judah.
2 Chronicles 20:3

CHAPTER 8

Tests In Your Singleness

There are many tests you will endure during your singleness that will reveal your level of faith and your strength of endurance to live fully for God. The purpose of this chapter is to prepare you for the tests and boost your confidence knowing that with the grace of God you can pass each and every test.

In prior chapters of this book I have provided examples of how Satan desires to lure you as a single woman into the traps of lust, fornication, and impatience and how he desires to weaken your faith by believing that God has forgotten about you and that you will never see your prayers for marriage answered. This chapter emphasizes the tests of the heart; and your willingness to be obedient to the move of the Holy Spirit and to God's plan for your life in the midst of your singleness – even when things don't make sense.

TESTS ARE NECESSARY

You should know that your desire for marriage is a good desire. God created marriage, He loves marriage and therefore sanctifies marriages; marriages are a blessing to His Kingdom, so never feel guilty or ashamed of your desire for marriage. God said He will gives us the desires of our hearts when we delight in Him (Psalm 37:4), so as you pray for marriage and believe God for marriage, it is important that you trust Him for the manifestation of marriage without it becoming an idol in your life. Remember, our God is a jealous God and just as He instructed us through the 10 commandments there should be no other gods before Him. God wants to be first and will use tests during your singleness to ensure that He is the priority in your life.

During my singleness, I had conquered many of the tests concerning my flesh. I had warred through prayer and fasting to bring my flesh (finally) into submission, and no longer felt the urge or desire to have sex with men that were not my husband or drink alcohol. God had delivered me from the temptations of the flesh, however I still had to overcome tests concerning my heart. During this testing time of my life, I was very involved in my church and believing God passionately for a husband. I was filled with the Holy Spirit and doing my best to be patient and wait on God so I filled much of my time with being active in my church and attending as many church services as possible. So when a friendship with a young minister from my mother's church blossomed into a budding romance, I was excited at the prospect.

We had much in common. He was a few years younger than I, however he was mature and intent on doing the work of God. I had known of him through my work in politics and we worked out at the same gym. We became close, after he learned of my recent completion of a half-marathon; he asked would I help train him for his upcoming race. I agreed to help him in his endeavors, and set up a weekly training regime, which included 6:00 am morning runs. Our thrice-weekly runs evolved from general conversation about the weather and upcoming day's events to times of prayer, testimony and basking in the presence of God as we watched the sun rise over the downtown skyline.

I was beginning to like the young minister and couldn't help but wonder, *"Lord, is he the ONE?"* According to my mental checklist, he appeared to posses everything that I was looking for in a godly man. From the looks of it, it seemed as if God's hand was supernaturally weaving us together. We ended up dating for about a year. We attended family gatherings together, supported each other at church services and ministry opportunities. We studied the word of God together, we prayed and confided with one another. I was confident that I had received God's stamp of approval on this relationship with the young minister. God had finally answered prayers for a husband, and as time progressed we began to gingerly discuss our next steps and future, including marriage.

Prayer does work, I thought with satisfaction. I was in love and I knew that the young minister loved me. He was kind, caring, and compassionate and treated me well. We had made the decision we would honor God through our relationship and we kept ourselves sexually pure. I felt relaxed in the relationship. I was satisfied. I had prayed and God had answered my prayers by sending me a talented and anointed young minister that would soon become my husband. Unfortunately, I would quickly and abruptly learn, that despite things appearing wonderful, God would require me to walk a hard path of obedience and end this relationship.

WARNINGS DURING THE TEST

If I look back, I can see that God did provide warning signs in the relationship with the young minister. There was his hesitancy and pensive support as I delved deeper into God's word and in the life of ministry. When we first met for our daily runs, I was a baby Christian. I looked up to him because he knew so much about God's word; however, as God began to work through me and call me into ministry, he confided his hesitancy and concern about having a potential wife that would also preach the gospel.

Yes, he wanted a godly wife, but he didn't necessarily want a wife that also preached. He was content with his wife teaching Sunday school, or ministering on special occasions, but ultimately, he wanted a wife that would support him and encourage him in his own ministry endeavors. I ignored his concerns, figuring God would deal with his heart. I was satisfied that for now, he supported me in my Sunday school teaching,

74

and Friday evening Bible classes. For now, his level of support was good enough. I ignored the possibility of what would lie in the future as God continued to advance me in ministry.

God then sent His messenger, by the name of Prophet Brian Carn to warn me of my relationship with the young minister. Prophet Brian Carn, a nationally known and respected prophet was in my hometown for a three-night revival. It was the first night of the church service, and through the word of knowledge, he called me by first name from the audience. There were at least 500 people in attendance for the service, and I was excited, nervous and a bit bewildered as to how he knew my name, and what message did he have from God for me.

Prophet Carn prophetically ministered and flowed heavily in God's anointing that night. He told me of God's plans for me to write books that would bless the Body of Christ. He also revealed things about my childhood, and current struggles in a new job that could only have been revealed by God. These were things that many people didn't know, things that I didn't share with anyone, let alone a visiting Prophet. This is why God's word says that He does reveal the secret things to His Prophets. (Amos 3:7) God sent Prophet Brian Carn to minister to me personally, first through the word of knowledge, to elevate my faith, and then to later receive the devastating news he would soon share.

"You need to wait for God to send you the right man into your life. When the right man appears in your life, you will know he is from God. For one, he will not take away from you. Instead he will pour into you. Secondly, he will support the call of God on your life. He won't try to quench it nor will he be envious or try to downplay it. He will support you in ministry. Wait, on God. He will send you the type of man you need."

After speaking these words, Prophet Carn laid hands on me, and I fell in the Spirit. As I lay on the floor at the altar, I contemplated the words of the Prophet.

Wait on God? Why was he telling me to wait for a man? God had already sent me a man. I had already waited and God has rewarded me for waiting....in fact, I waited so well he sent me a young minister. Why is Prophet Carn telling me to wait on God? What does he mean?

By then end of the church service, I concluded that the things Prophet Carn ministered to me about my life – my childhood, my desire to write books and current issues at work were correct. However, he was wrong – dead wrong concerning God's will for me to wait for a godly man to enter into my life. God had already sent a great man into my life, and so I foolishly disregarded the Prophet's words concerning the young minister and plowed forward in the relationship.

My decision to be disobedient and ignore the instruction sent by Prophet Carn did not deter God from sending another messenger. This time God sent a woman my way. She was an Apostle over a small church and operated very strongly in the gift of prophecy. We decided to meet for dinner, and as I shared my plans about marrying the young minister, she abruptly stated that the young minister was not God's choice for my husband.

She continued that God understood how I loved the young minister. However, he was not God's best choice as a husband for me. Instead of receiving her words, I became insulted and offended. I disregarded her remarks as jealousy, and rolled my eyes at her outrageous claim that the young minister was not God's best. *How could my boyfriend not be God's best?* I had dated many men who neglected to measure halfway to the young minister's spirituality, I scoffed.

The young minister loved me, he treated me well, he was earnest, faithful, and called by God. Of course he was God's best. After all, if he wasn't God's best, why would He allow the relationship to continue? My ears were deafened to the heeding and instruction by God's messengers. God, nevertheless remained undeterred. He eventually got my attention using a woman 5'5 in height to get in my face at a prayer breakfast and blatantly speak what God was saying to me about my future with the young minister.

My encounter with the 5'5 woman happened less than three weeks after my encounter with Prophet Brian Carn. It took place at a prophetic prayer breakfast led by Elder Deborah Blissett-Arnold in St. Louis, Missouri. The service had been high all morning with worship, and praise. Throughout the service, as I worshipped God, I couldn't help but notice this strange short woman praising God, yet in between her praise, she would intermittently scowl, point her fingers and wave her fists at the air. It was as if she was pointing at demons and taking authority in the spirit realm.

As the service came to a close, my spiritual mother, the fiery Apostle Barbara J. McClain, released a last minute prophetic word to the tiny 5'5 woman for the crowd to hear. Apostle McClain requested that I serve as her prophetic scribe by recording the prophecy for the diminutive woman. After the prophetic word was issued and I presented the hand-written notes of the prophetic word that was released to the 5'5 woman, our hands touched, and upon contact she began to prophesy to me.

As she began to prophesy she started with a scripture that had been repeatedly spoken over my life during that season 1 Corinthians 2:9 *"No eye has seen, no ear has heard what God has in store for those who love Him."* Her speaking this scripture grabbed my attention. She confirmed much of what I had heard before. She spoke to God using me to write books and travel the world. She spoke of great things God had in store for me in ministry. She appeared as if she was going to stop, so I politely thanked her and began to collect my things to leave, but then she grabbed me and moved directly in my face and said:

"The man you are with is not the man God has for you. You need to get out of that relationship now! God has someone that He has created just for you, and if you stay with this man, you are going to miss the special one God has for you."

I couldn't process her words. What exactly was she saying?

She moved even closer to me to make sure that I heard her.

"Do you hear me? Do you understand what I am saying to you? You need to get out of this relationship and you need to do it now! God has a Boaz for you – and you are about to miss him staying with this man that you are with!"

As she spoke louder and louder, I turned from her because I did not want to hear anymore. What did she mean that the young minister was not the man God had chosen? Get out of the relationship now? And who was this other person God had for me? I was upset and confused, however the 5'5 lady would not let me go. As I twisted in my chair to turn away from her, she turned with me, got in my face and continued speaking, this time harshly, *"You will be sorry if you stay in this relationship.*

You will not get to where God is trying to take you if you remain. You will be hindered. I know it hurts but you need to listen to me! You need to get out now."

I was devastated. I thought about just completely ignoring the short woman but another part wanted to hear more. *Who was she? Could this be true? Hadn't God ordained my relationship with the young minister? Were we not doing everything right? How could this not be the right relationship God had for me?* Even though I didn't want to accept the words of the woman, I knew deep down inside she was right. How did I know she was right? The Lord brought to my memory all the discussions the young minister and I had regarding ministry and his insecurities and hesitancy regarding my advancement in ministry.

The Lord then brought the faces of the three prophets, His messengers he had sent to release the word to me. I then realized that I had been so focused on moving forward in the relationship with the young minister, settling down and getting married, that I had closed my ears to God; preventing me from hearing directly from Him. Therefore He used His messengers to ensure I did not miss his message, that it was not His will for me to marry the young minister.

YOU MUST MAKE A CHOICE

I had a choice to make. This was a test that God had led me to. Would I obey and heed His instruction carried by His prophets or would ignore, and continue to move based on what I wanted to do? As I exited the prayer breakfast, I cried and I prayed and I prayed and I cried. My heart felt heavy. It seemed as if I was so close to having my desires met by God, by being in a relationship with a godly man, who loved and treated me well, but now God was pulling the rug from under my feet, and telling me that the relationship was not in His will. I was confused. I was angry.

God, do you want me single forever? I cried

As I drove home, I heard the Lord whisper, *"Just trust me."* I rolled my eyes. I angry and upset at God, *Why did He let me get to the point of even discussing marriage with the young minister, when He knew it would never work in the end?* Despite my eye-rolling and anger, I knew that I had to trust God It would be fruitless to try and pursue a relationship when God had spoken so plainly that it was not His will.

That evening, I met with the young minister and ended our relationship. It was a difficult conversation on many levels, however, I knew it was the right thing to do, and eventually he understood it as well. Many people ask, how I knew to trust God in a situation such as this, and my only answer is that at the end of the day, I just wanted to be obedient to God. Even though I loved the young minister, and of course wanted to get married and live a happy, simple life with him; I believed

81

the word of God sent through His Prophets. And because I believed His word, I knew I had to end the relationship. This was my test of obedience during my singleness.

My experience with the young minister taught me that some relationships can be good, quality relationships. However, that does not mean they are God's best. The young minister and I were good with each other, but we were not God's best for each other. God desires for you to marry His best, and He knows exactly what we need in regards to His best. Once the young minister and I agreed to end our relationship, God later provided confirmation after confirmation that we made the right choice. The young minister is now pursuing a degree in divinity at a local seminary, he is preaching the gospel and from what I hear is doing very well in life.

TRUST GOD DURING THE TEST

God wants to know if He has your heart, and by having His heart, will you will trust Him even when you can't trace Him? Many of the prophetic words that were spoken in my life after my relationship with the young minister, stated that God had someone custom made just for me. A great man of God that would love me as I desired to be loved, and would pour into me and support me in ministry. After my relationship with the young minister, I had no idea who this new guy would be, and honestly, on some days still sulked and felt angry towards God. My wounded heart told God that I didn't want this "new" guy.

The young minister would have been just fine, and *to just leave me alone in regards to my singleness.* At the time I couldn't fathom being in another relationship and undergoing a potential heartbreak. Looking back now, I recall how that year of waiting was marked by an encounter with God where He showed me unconditional love. When I whined and complained about what I'd lost and spewed my bitter words regarding my heartbreak, God loved me through it. In fact He loved my life back to alignment with His way, so that eventually the bitterness began to wane and then disappear. I began to look forward to the *new* thing God had for my life.

Everyone's tests are different, but know that whatever God requires you to give up, He will bless you with something much greater. Tests require courage and obedience. While you are in the midst of the test know that God is rooting for you and will help you every step along the way. Remember, the great thing about passing tests is that you always receive a favorable reward. In this example, we can look at the life of Abraham, and see how this father of faith, was rewarded for his obedience and willingness to follow God by moving from his homeland and relocating to an unknown land. We also can see how he was rewarded based upon his willingness to sacrifice his son Isaac. God rewarded Abraham for passing these many tests. Make the decision that regardless of what tests lie before you in your singleness that you will pass them. After all, it is for His glory and every passed test is simply a steeping stone to bring you closer to your destiny.

83

Prayer

Lord, please give me the wisdom, and the strength to pass every test that comes my way. I know that through your Holy Spirit you will guide and bless me and show me how to navigate my way my through the twists and turns of life. God, open my ears so I may hear your voice. Your word says, your sheep know your voice. Prevent me from being sidetracked where I would lose focus and become distracted from hearing and heeding your direction. I thank you God that through every test and storm you are with me, and that I have the victory. In Jesus' name, Amen.

The Heart of God

The seed falling on rocky ground refers to someone who hears the word and at once receives it with joy. But since they have no root, they last only a short time. When trouble or persecution comes because of the word, they quickly fall away.

Matthew 13:20-21

Consider it pure joy, my brothers and sisters whenever you face trials of many kinds, because you know that the testing of your faith produces perseverance. Let perseverance finish its work so that you may be mature and complete, not lacking anything.

James 1:2-4

See, I have refined you, though not as silver. I have tested you in the furnace of affliction.

Isaiah 48:10

CHAPTER 9

Date with Purpose

There will come a time when a man will state his interest in you and begin pursuing you. You can expect all types of emotions ranging from excitement, nervousness and even a bit of anxiety. These are all normal feelings, and are all part of the process of moving from singleness to marriage. God desires us to have fun and to enjoy life, in fact that is part of the reason Jesus came to Earth; to save us from sins and for us to live an abundant life. (John 10:10).

Life is more than just church, prayer and work. God has created the need within us for companionship and for quality relationships. It is perfectly okay to date, however do so with purpose, standards and boundaries to ensure you do not fall victim to the traps set by the enemy.

HAVE FUN, BE ALERT

When Jesus sent his disciples out to witness, he encouraged them to be "as shrewd as snakes and as innocent as doves." (Matthew 10:16) Whether you date regularly or haven't been out on a date in a long time, when the opportunity comes, enjoy yourself however keep your wits by being sober, and vigilant. During the courtship with my husband, I enjoyed every moment. It was fun putting together my outfits, primping and fussing over my hair, and just spending carefree hours with him in courtship. We truly had a summer romance that was blissful, exciting and romantic. I don't think I laughed so much in my life, and the good thing is that I am still laughing...

PURPOSEFUL DATING

As men pursue you, it is important that you date with intentionality. Avoid dating someone just because they asked or because they have expressed interest. In fact, you should have your mind set that you will only date men who are compatible with where God is taking you spiritually. 2 Corinthians 6:14 says, "Do not be yoked with unbelievers." As a woman who is anointed and seeking a Kingdom marriage, don't even waste your time with a man that does not have a personal relationship with Christ. Also, avoid dating several men at one time. Dating or courtship is an opportunity for you to get to know a person; it is not the time for you to fling from one relationship to another.

Use dating as a time to intentionally get to know a person. Use the time of dating to inspect the fruit of the spirit to see if they are evident in his life. What kind of spiritual fruit does his tree produce? Is the fruit fresh and ripe or is it spoiled and rotten? Jesus told His disciples that they would know His messengers by their fruit (Matthew 7:16). As God's daughter, and an heir of His royal priesthood, you want to be yoked with a man of God that has already established a track record of submitting to Christ. Refuse to waste your time, as Ephesians 5:15-16 instructs us to make the "most of every opportunity, because the days are evil." As a woman after God's own heart, you don't have time to waste with men who are not intentional after the things of God.

HAVE GODLY STANDARDS

After so many false starts, I began to ask God to hide me from every counterfeit and random man that would derail me from my purpose and destiny in Him. I was tired of getting my hopes up, tired of wondering if this guy was "the one." I simply wanted to glean in the fields of ministry, like Ruth uninhibited until it was time to encounter my Boaz. I didn't want to be bothered with dates that would lead to nowhere, nor was I interested in developing relationships with multiple men.

After my last relationship with the young minister, God answered my prayers and I was completely hidden until God revealed me to my husband. For a season, my phone didn't ring, men didn't stop and ask me my name, they didn't ask me about the weather -- it was if I was invisible, which was totally fine with me. I had reached the point where my ego was no longer fed by the catcalls and "hey baby's" by random men. I only wanted to pique the interest of the man that would be my husband. I used this time to intentionally pray about the type of man that I desired to marry.

The man would have to be someone who was active in church and ministry. I knew that God was calling me into ministry, and so my husband would also need to have that same call. He would also need to be accepting and supportive of the purpose that God had ordained for my life. I felt confident that God would reveal this man to me, I had assurance from God through my prayers, and also took comfort in the many prophetic words that I received from individuals that would encourage me to wait on God for my husband and that indeed he would be worth the wait.

As a single woman you want to have your standards for a mate defined, so you do not get seduced or tricked by the enemy and settle for a counterfeit. Is the man you date someone you can imagine becoming one with? Ephesians 5:31 states that the husband will leave his father and mother to join you and become one flesh. As you date and get to know the man pursuing you, you should begin to think of these things and ask God to show you if this is the man with whom you will become one.

MEETING BOAZ

When I finally met my husband and participated in a few weeks of dating, we knew without a doubt that it was God's desire for us to marry. We immediately sought the blessing of our families and also the blessing of our spiritual leaders. We then moved forward with pre-marital counseling. Many people ask me, how did I know that my husband was "the one"? I respond simply that the Holy Spirit informed me. God set his plan in motion a few days prior to being introduced to my husband by having it prophesied through a prayer line.

I was on a prayer line with a young lady, named Ebony Pollard that I had recently met. Through prayer, she began to minister prophetically. She excitedly told me that something I had been praying about for a long time was due to materialize in just a few days. *"Kacie, it is just days away!"* she exclaimed. I knew that she was talking about meeting my husband. God had given me several dreams confirming that my husband was near, and my prayer for a godly marriage had been on my prayer list for many years. I was excited yet I was also a bit weary. I was in the midst of recovering from an intense spiritual battle, due to a very public and humiliating scandal that had resulted from my job in politics and my spirit felt forlorn and weak. In other words, I was tired. I had been unemployed for several months as a result of the scandal and unable to gain traction in any area of my life – my ministry seemed to be stagnant, my finances were at an all time low, and bills were piling up all around me. I was experiencing hard times.

After the prayer call with Ebony, I simply prayed to God, *"Let your will be done."* Three days later, I received a message on Facebook from a handsome gentleman named Alfred Long. I knew of Alfred primarily as an advertiser on my local Christian radio show. He had purchased advertising packages from time to time, however we had never communicated outside his advertising needs. Through his Facebook message, he stated simply how the Lord had been leading him to pray for me, and he wasn't sure why he was praying for me, but he was simply being obedient to the spirit of the Lord, and he wanted to let me know.

The moment I read Al's message, the Holy Spirit nudged my spirit and said, *"He is the one."*

It was a soft voice. Very gentle that brought both a sense of calmness and peace into my heart. I believed the Holy Spirit, yet fear and doubt crawled its way into my thoughts. *How did I know for sure that this was the Holy Spirit and not just my flesh? How could I be so sure that he was the one? Hadn't I thought that so many times before?* If this was truly the man the Lord had for me, God was going to have to show me in other ways outside of this "feeling" I had deep in my spirit. I was tired. Curious, but tired. Tired of getting my hopes up. Tired of false starts and dashed hopes.

Later that evening, I decided to step out on faith and embark upon trying to learn more about Alfred. I knew that he was involved in prison ministry from his many Facebook posts and so I messaged him to ask if he would be willing to help me coordinate an upcoming ministry event inside a women's prison near Kansas City, MO.

Alfred jumped on the opportunity and suggested he take me to dinner to discuss. It was during our dinner that we eventually coined as our first date, that I learned Al was an associate minister and had been involved in ministry for over 30 years. He was the father of three adult children, two grandchildren and was twice divorced. He was also 28 years older than me. Doing the math, Al was the same age of my deceased father and one year older than my mother.

His past marital background nor age didn't bother or fluster me. The reason why these things didn't bother me, is a year earlier I had received several prophetic words at various church services, that my husband would be much older and would possess the wisdom and godly characteristics that I needed. (I am so thankful that God thought enough of me to give me clear clues of what my husband would look like and the qualities he would possess. Had I not received several confirming words regarding His age, I probably would have missed my Boaz!)

As we dated, God provided peace in my spirit and along with tangible confirmation time and time again that Al was indeed the husband he had custom made for me. There were things God had revealed to me about my husband, many years ago during my time of journaling, prayer and fasting; that Al would speak upon, or confide that reminded me what God said concerning my future husband.

Al was gracious, kind and God-fearing. He loved the Lord and was on fire for Him. He loved me, He honored me and treated me like a queen. He spoke life into me and during one of the roughest times in my life, when I often felt like a wilted flower; Al ministered and refreshed me through encouragement, kindness and compassion. It wasn't hard to fall in love with him. During our courtship, I told often told him that he made loving him easy, and he still does. God blessed us throughout our courtship, and just like Ruth, I (finally) met my real life Boaz.

SET BOUNDARIES

Al and I established standards and boundaries in our relationship to ensure that we would honor God with our bodies. For example we were sure to avoid extended times where we would be alone and tempted to have sex. Both of us were passionate about each other, and God made sure we kept ourselves pure by having model chaperones though Al's youngest adult daughter, Tamar and granddaughter, Kennedi who lived with him during that time. They served as extra security for us. It was also important for our good not to be spoken evil of, so I didn't venture to his bedroom. His bedroom was sacred and off limits to me, these were personal boundaries that I established, I figured I would see it once we got married.

During our date nights, because his sole TV was located in the bedroom, we plugged our laptops in the front room and watched movies using Netflix where we could be out in the open and held accountable. As his future wife, it was important that I did my best to protect and cover him. I didn't want to compromise his anointing, by contributing or aiding in his sexual downfall. Just as much as I cared about wanting to remain pure and clean before God, I felt the same protection towards him. I I always made sure I was dolled up and looked attractive during our time together, however, I was careful to never seduce him or cause him to fall into temptation through my clothes or language. I honored Al through our courtship and he did the same for me.

The boundaries and standards we established in our courtship help set the foundation for a strong and stable marriage built on the principles of honoring and placing God first. Dating is exciting, it's fun and can be a whirlwind experience, however, know that as a Christian woman, you want to engage in this important step with the heart and mind of Christ, heeding His direction and yielding to His spirit.

Prayer

Dear God,

Give me wisdom for this season of my life. As you open the door of dating to me, show me when to say 'yes' and when to say 'no' to those who seek to distract or re-route me from my plan and purpose in you. I ask that you protect me from those who Satan may send as counterfeits and imposters to the true man you have ordained for me. Give me great wisdom and discernment in this season to see beyond the natural and inspect and evaluate the spiritual fruit. I thank you Lord that I seek you for truth. I trust you and believe in you, and I thank you for being with me every step of the way, even when dating. In Jesus' name. Amen.

The Heart of God

Do two walk together unless they have agreed to do so.
Amos 3:3

But among you there must not even be a hint of sexual immorality, or any kind of impurity or greed because these are improper for God's holy people.
Ephesians 5:3

Be very careful, then how you live – not as unwise but as wise, making the most of every opportunity, because the days are evil.
Ephesians 5:15-16

Therefore do not let what you know is good be spoken of as evil.
Romans 14:16

CHAPTER 10

The Blessings of Singleness

Your time of singleness is a wonderful time of blessing and favor from God. God desires for you to open your eyes and see this season of your life from His perspective and receive the blessings He has stored just for you in this season. Do you see how God's hand is upon your life, even in your singleness? Do you see how He has provided and protected you throughout your singleness? Regardless of how you have come upon singleness whether through a divorce, the death of a spouse or having never been married, God longs for you to appreciate where you are now with gratitude and praise and then thank Him for where He's taking you.

By now, you know that for so long I wanted out of my singleness. I prayed, cried, whined and pouted about being single, but none of that compelled God to move any faster on my behalf to bringing me a husband. God brings us into our destiny according to His own time. Our responsibility is to know that He is not slow concerning His promises, He just simply gives us time to come into repentance. (2 Peter 3:8)

It may seem as if God is dragging His feet in your life, but God is doing much more than that. He is working spiritually, on things you can't see. God cares much more about you than just granting you a husband. He's most concerned about your heart and ensuring that you have a solid relationship with Him. Your solid relationship with Him is what will strengthen your marriage and sustain you as a wife.

RESTORATION IN SINGLENESS

This entire book has been about making sure the fundamentals of your heart and relationship are in place first before God grants you marriage. So often we get the order twisted, but God desires to raise up godly women who have His heart and a relationship with Him to then bless and marry sons after His own heart. Don't neglect the blessings God has for you right now as a single woman. It was through my singleness that I learned what it meant to have faith, even when situations in my life seemed impossible. For the last portion of my singleness, I went through an embarrassing public scandal that caused me to lose my job, endure a reputation in tatters, live as an adult woman at home with her mother without any stable income. Satan taunted me, *"Who would want you for a wife?"* He sneered.

It was these lessons I had learned earlier in my time of singleness: the fasting, the prayers of warfare against the enemy, the faith in God's Word that I relentlessly held on to during hours of prayer and personal study that allowed me to combat the enemy's lies and condemnation. I was able to remind Satan what God's word said concerning me. That despite the mistakes I had made and the current situation I found myself in, God had a "good plan and purpose for my life" (Jeremiah 29:11) and despite what the situation looked like now, in the end "all things were going to work together for my good." (Romans 8:28).

This is a powerful example of how the blessings I encountered during my singleness prepared me to be stronger and more mature in my Christian walk. The loneliness I endured, the times when it seemed as if I had nowhere to turn, no friend to talk to, all these instances led me to the One who always had time for me. The One who always provided me a listening ear and welcomed me with His loving arms. The blessings that manifested from my time of singleness also taught me that God is a restorer and a relationship with Him produces benefits.

You've heard of "friends with benefits" but the type of benefits that come from having a relationship with God are everlasting and eternal. My relationship with God allowed Him to forgive all my sins and transform me from the pit of destruction to receive a crown of loving kindness (Psalm 10:2-4).

The majority of my singleness consisted of a life of sin – heavy drinking, fornication, adultery, pornography, lies and manipulation; however in spite of this, God came in and rescued me. He transformed my life, my heart and my thought patterns. Regardless of what you have done in your singleness, once you submit your life to Jesus, He can truly redeem and restore you.

SINGLNESS IS NECESSARY

Your time of singleness is necessary. This is a blessed time of preparation, purification and a time of greater intimacy with our heavenly Father. I remember one day a friend asked me, *"Well, why do you think you are still single?"* At this time I was hosting a Christian talk show, speaking at various churches and living truly for God. In response to his question, I simply shrugged my shoulders and stated that I was ready for a husband. I was simply waiting on God.

My reply arrogantly implied that I had done all my work and I was simply waiting on God to finish his part. The Lord revealed after this conversation, that the spirit of pride had settled in my heart. Yes, I had come a long way, but it was through His grace. I felt that I was ready to be a wife, but the reason why I wasn't a wife was because there were some things that God still needed to work out in me; particularly pride.

A blessing of my singleness was the time God provided that was uninterrupted "he and I" time. God allowed this precious time to chisel things out of me that would prevent me from reaching my destiny. Just as God did for me, He is doing the same thing for you. You may feel in your heart that you are ready and are simply "waiting on God," however God has you right where you need to be. He is still getting you ready and working on the areas you can't see. Accept God's plan and accept His roadmap and timeline for your life. When you accept and submit to God's plan then you can truly enjoy the blessings of singleness and your Christian journey.

The blessings I learned during my singleness are what prepared me to be a wife to my husband. The lessons on patience, faith, contentment, fasting and prayer, along with enduring and passing the tests posed during my singleness are what led me to the loving and saved arms of my husband, Mr. Alfred T. Long, Sr! God desires to bless you with your heart's desires but He first wants to ensure that He is your *first* desire. When He is your first desire you won't have to ask in exasperation, *"God, Where is My Husband?"* You will instead acknowledge that God is moving in His own way and according to His own timetable. His word is true and He will do exactly what He said He would do.

"This is the confidence we have in approaching God: that if we ask anything according to His will, He hears us. And if we know that He hears us – whatever we ask – we know that we have what we asked of Him." – 1 John 5:14-15

Prayer

Lord, let me not miss the blessings you have for me right in the midst of my singleness. Open my eyes and allow me to see how there are angels all around me. Help me to not complain nor grow weary, instead help me to see and receive your strength operating on the inside of me. Use me for your glory. May I be like the light shining on top of the hill for all to see. Open doors where I may go and witness for your glory. I make the commitment to serve you, to honor you and put you first in everything I do. I love you and I give glory to you in your precious son's name, Jesus Christ. Amen.

The Heart of God

I have loved you with an everlasting love, therefore I have
continued by faithfulness to you.
Jeremiah 31:3

But seek first his kingdom and his righteousness, and all these
things will be given to you as well.
Matthew 6:33

And Elisha prayed, "Open his eyes, LORD, so that he may
see." Then the LORD opened the servant's eyes, and he looked
and saw
2 Kings 6:17a

Bonus Chapter: While Single Don't Forget Your P's

By Min. Alfred T. Long, Sr.

*"I remember that warm summer evening in June when we first met…
it was supposed to be a ministry meeting. 6:00pm and I was there
sharp not knowing what to expect but expecting something, I just
didn't know what. And Baby you walked in that joint and BAM! My
heart started beating fast, I broke out in a slight sweat in that air-
conditioned restaurant, but I played it cool because this was a ministry
meeting…right? As we talked your beauty intoxicated me as I listened
closely to your words; because somehow deep in my spirit I knew my
destiny was clothed in that red dress wrapped in a chocolate six feet of
God's wonderful creativity. But I played it cool, real cool though my
heart was thumping and my mind was racing to come up with a plan
to see you again. That evening at dinner we talked about everything
but ministry and I felt I had known you all of my life."*

Ha! Those were part of my wedding vows to Kacie and they
describe our first meeting. I know scripture says "He that finds
a wife finds a good thing and favor from God." (Proverbs 18:22)
The funny thing for me was I actually came to discuss business.
I was exiting a long-term relationship with a really good woman

and wasn't looking for a wife. But my Father knows best right? As we talked over dinner that evening getting to know each other I kind of subconsciously started checking off attributes of what I wanted in a wife. If you asked me why, I couldn't tell you. My mental checklist looked liked this:

- Is she saved and does she mention how much she loves God in her conversation?
- Does she attend Church regularly?
- Is she in ministry?
- Does she gossip or talk negatively about Church?
- Is she a giver?
- Can she hold her own in an intelligent conversation?
- Is she involved in community service?
- Does she look me in the eye when she talks?
- Is she polite to the service people?
- Does she work out?

Kacie skated through my mental checklist with flying colors! I started paying closer attention to Kacie as I realized I might be staring at my destiny. I couldn't help but notice her physical beauty when I first laid eyes on her but I knew that physical beauty was temporary and I needed that spiritual connection. It was there! After I left that meeting my mind was in a whirlwind and I thought my emotions were playing tricks on me. This was too intense and too fast for me. But God knew what He was doing. I was reminded of a song by Smokey Robinson, "One

Heartbeat". This is the first stanza of the lyrics from that song:

"Two hearts, two of a kind
Love at first sight, why do they say love is blind?
Slow down, we don't have to move fast
Cause the love that is real is made to last".

As I write this Kacie and I are celebrating three months of marriage. Proverbs 27:17 teaches us that as iron sharpens iron a friend sharpens their friend. In our relationship God is molding two very independent people into a team, a partnership for His glory. Part of our covenant and prayer for our marriage is that God make us one in spirit, soul and body. And it's an adventure everyday to see how God is answering our prayer! As I conclude my chapter I'd like to share some simple advice for those of you (male and female) seeking and praying for that special person God has for you in marriage.

I call them the 4 P's:

1.) Prayer – allow God to remove any anxiety you may have concerning a mate. (Philippians 4:6)

"Do not fret or have any anxiety about anything, but in every circumstance and in everything, by prayer and petition (definite requests), with thanksgiving, continue to make your wants known to God".

2.) Persistence – keep praying even when circumstances
   seem dim and your potential mate is nowhere in sight.
(Luke 18:1)
"Also [Jesus] told them a parable to the effect that they ought
always to pray and not to turn coward (faint, lose heart, and
give up)".

3.) Preparation – allow the Holy Spirit to cut all soul ties
   from previous relationships and to remove any emotional
   baggage you may bring into a marriage.
(Philippians 3:13)
"I do not consider, brethren, that I have captured and made
it my own [yet]; but one thing I do [it is my one aspiration]:
forgetting what lies behind and straining forward to what lies
ahead".

4.) Praise – when loneliness tries to creep in praise God that,
   not only is God preparing you for your mate, but also
   He's preparing your mate for you.
(1 Thessalonians 5:18)
"Thank [God] in everything [no matter what the circumstances
may be, be thankful and give thanks], for this is the will of God
for you [who are] in Christ Jesus [the Revealer and Mediator of
that will]".

As I finish this chapter I'm listening to Gospel music and
relaxing with my wife. And I can say Kacie Starr Long was
worth the wait. Thank You Lord for your favor!

110

Prayer of Salvation

If you haven't accepted Jesus in your heart, now would be the perfect time to do so. Remember more than anything, God desires to have a relationship with you first. Below is the prayer of salvation that Al and I included in our wedding program. If you have said this prayer for the first time after reading this book, I would love to hear your testimony. Blessings to you and welcome to a life in Jesus Christ!

Dear God in heaven, I come to you in the name of Jesus. I acknowledge that I am a sinner, and I am sorry for my sins and the life that I have lived; I need your forgiveness. I believe that your only begotten Son Jesus Christ shed His precious blood on the cross at Calvary and died for my sins, and I am now willing to turn from my sin.

You said in your Holy Word, Romans 10:9 that if we confess the Lord our God and believe in our hearts that God raised Jesus from the dead, we shall be saved. Right now I confess Jesus as the Lord of my soul. With my heart, I believe that you raised Jesus from the dead. This very moment I accept Jesus Christ as my own personal Savior and according to His Word, right now I am saved.

Lord Jesus, transform my life so that I may bring glory and honor to you alone for the rest of my life. Amen.

To contact Kacie write:

Inspired Overflow Ministries
P.O. Box 2408
Florissant, MO 63032

Email: Kacie@InspiredOverflow.com
Website: www.InspiredOverflow.com

We would love to hear your testimony on how you have received help from this book. Your prayer requests are also welcome.

67894264R00074

Made in the USA
Lexington, KY
25 September 2017